Smoothi

Triathletes

Recipes and Nutrition Plan to Support Triathlon Training from Sprint to Ironman and Beyond (Food for Fitness Series)

Lars Andersen

Published by Nordic Standard Publishing

Atlanta, Georgia USA

ISBN 978-1-484192-71-9

9 781484 192719 >

Lars Andersen

Copyright © 2012 Lars Andersen

What Our Readers Are Saying

"I've really started to notice a positive difference in my performance since starting this program"

★★★★☆ **Vincent K. Vogl (Perry, IL)**

"Had all of the information I needed to get started so I had no more excuses not to train"

★★★★☆ **Michael S. Leto (Concord, MA)**

"Great sport-specific nutrition advice and information. Perfect"

★★★★★ **Gregory L. Small (Sacramento, CA)**

2

Exclusive Bonus Download: Athletic Training

Always wanted to be a world class athlete? Here is everything you need to know on how to reach the peaks of performance!

Do you ever envy those people who are ace athletes without appearing to put any effort into it at all?

Without the right tools and information, it could take you years to figure out the secrets to achieving peak performance. Instead of spending a fortune on so-called experts or knocking yourself out with the old trial and error method, there is an easier way to learn how to achieve success in athletics the way you've always dreamed.

Introducing... Athletic Training!

Everything you need to know about becoming a great athlete is included in this special report:

- Secrets to peak performance

- Achieving balance
- Purpose and performance
- Planning
- Training regimens
- Goal setting
- Training your whole body
- Strength training

I leave absolutely nothing out! Everything that I learned in order to improve to learn how to become an ace athlete, I show you.

No stone is left unturned in this comprehensive report! You won't want to miss out on this!

CLICK HERE to download this guide and start achieving your weight loss and fitness goals NOW

Thank you for downloading my book. Please REVIEW this book on Amazon. I need your feedback to make the next version better. Thank you so much!

Books by Lars Andersen

The Smoothies for Runners Book

Juices for Runners

Smoothies for Cyclists

Juices for Cyclists

Paleo Diet for Cyclists

Smoothies for Triathletes

Juices for Triathletes

Paleo Diet for Triathletes

Smoothies for Strength

Juices for Strength

Paleo Diet for Strength

Paleo Diet Smoothies for Strength

Smoothies for Golfers

Juices for Golfers

Table of Contents

PRE-RACE SMOOTHIES - FOR RACES LASTING 4 OR MORE HOURS

POST-RACE SMOOTHIES

Disclaimer

While all attempts have been made to provide effective, verifiable information in this Book, neither the Author nor Publisher assumes any responsibility for errors, inaccuracies, or omissions. Any slights of people or organizations are unintentional.

This Book is not a source of medical information, and it should not be regarded as such. This publication is designed to provide accurate and authoritative information in regard to the subject matter covered. It is sold with the understanding that the publisher is not engaged in rendering a medical service. As with any medical advice, the reader is strongly encouraged to seek professional medical advice before taking action.

Smoothies for Triathletes

"If you set a goal for yourself and you are able to achieve it, you have won your race. Your goal can be to come in first, to improve your performance, or just finish the race it's up to you." - Dave Scott

Whether competing in sprint distance, Olympic distance, long distance or Ironman events, triathlon is a multi-discipline sport that requires a lot of energy. The foods you eat on a daily basis are your body's only source of energy so getting the right balance of nutrients is essential to fuel your performance.

Calculating Your Energy Needs

A balanced diet contains a healthy mix of carbohydrates, protein, fats, vitamins and minerals. The more physically active you are on a daily basis, the more calories you need.

A simple way to calculate your energy needs is to use the following equations:

Moderately active lifestyle – your body weight in pounds multiplied by 17.

For example, if you weigh 150 pounds and take part in "mini" triathlons for fun, training two or three times per week for less than two hours each time, your energy needs are 150 x 17 = 2550 calories per day.

Active lifestyle – your body weight in pounds multiplied by 20.

For example, if you weigh 150 pounds and compete regularly in Olympic distance triathlons, training five or more times each week for more than two hours each time at a moderate to high intensity, your energy needs are 150 x 20 = 3000 calories per day.

The foods you eat must fuel your body and your mind, keeping your muscles energized and your brain focused and alert. This means consuming quality, healthful calories. A fast food burger with regular fries and a shake offers around 1300 calories but they do not represent quality calories that will give your performance a boost. The optimal mix of nutrients needed to achieve a healthy balance in your diet is 60 percent carbohydrates, 30 percent fats and 10 percent protein. However, finding the time to prepare and eat healthful meals can be difficult when swimming, cycling and running training takes up much of your day. Smoothies provide a fast and efficient way to boost your daily intake of healthful calories, and to give your body and brain the fuel they need to perform at their best.

Fuelling Performance

Carbohydrates

Carbohydrates are described as "the athlete's best friend" as they provide the main source of energy to fuel performance. They can be split into two categories:

Simple carbohydrates - sources include:

Sugary foodstuffs such as candy, cakes and sodas

Honey, in the form of glucose

Fruits and vegetables, in the form fructose and sucrose

Milk and dairy products, in the form of lactose

Malted wheat and barley, sprouting grains and malt extract, in the form of maltose

Molasses, dextrose, corn syrup and invert syrup.

Complex carbohydrates - sources include:

Starchy foods such as bread and potatoes

Cereals

Pasta

Rice

All carbohydrates are converted by your body into glucose and glycogen before they can be used as fuel. Complex carbohydrates are broken down for use more slowly than simple carbohydrates, meaning they provide a slower release of energy. Whether you are swimming, cycling, or running, the working muscles are fuelled by glucose in the blood and by glycogen from stores in the liver and in the muscles. Glucose and glycogen are inter-convertible. When your body has a sufficient supply of glucose, carbohydrates are converted to glycogen and stored, but if glucose is in short supply, glycogen is converted to glucose ready for use.

Your body can only store enough glycogen for up to around two hours of intense exercise. Promoting maximum glycogen uptake is therefore of key importance in terms of fuelling performance. At the end of a training session, your body's ability to store glycogen is elevated. Eating carbohydrate-rich foods in this "glycogen window" of around 30 minutes after exercise is an effective way to replenish your glycogen stores, thereby boosting your energy levels for the rest of the day ... and keeping fuel in your tank for the next day!

Carbohydrate-rich smoothie ingredients include:

Fruits

The majority of fruits provide a relatively slow release of energy making them a good source of fuel for endurance sports such as triathlon. Fruits also provide an excellent source of antioxidants. Antioxidants protect your body against free radicals, chemicals which are produced in your body as part of its metabolism and defense against bacteria.

Strawberries - a rich source of vitamin C, an important antioxidant, and also an aid to the absorption of iron from vegetables.

Pears - a good source of vitamin C, potassium, pectin and bioflavonoids. Potassium plays a vital role in the healthy transmission of nerve impulses and also works with sodium to help maintain your body's fluid and electrolyte balance. Pectin provides fiber, and bioflavonoids are powerful antioxidants.

Mangoes - a good source of vitamin C and beta-carotene, the plant form of vitamin A, which helps to protect against free radicals.

Bananas - a rich source of potassium.

Kiwi fruit - a rich source of vitamin C and a good source of potassium.

Cherries - a good source of potassium and a useful source of vitamin C.

Apricots - a rich source of beta-carotene and vitamin C.

Blueberries - often described as "the ultimate brain food," blueberries have an antioxidant content of around five times higher than other fruits and vegetables. Research has discovered that a daily serving of 100 grams can stimulate new brain cell growth and slow down the effects of mental ageing. Mental sharpness can provide a "winning edge" during each transition, whether it's swim to cycle or cycle to run.

Vegetables

Vegetables also offer a healthful source of carbohydrates for energy and many vegetables contain health boosting vitamin, mineral and antioxidant properties. Dark green leafy vegetables are nutritionally-dense and ideal in green smoothies containing a mix of 60 percent fruits and 40 percent vegetables. The added fiber content helps to slow the absorption of sugar and thereby a slower and steadier release of energy is provided, helping to keep you physically and mentally alert for longer.

Cabbage - rich source of vitamin C, vitamin K, and a good source of vitamin E, potassium and beta-carotene. Vitamin K is essential in the formation of many proteins - the body's building blocks - and vitamin E has an important role to play in preventing free radical damage.

Broccoli - another rich source of vitamin C. Broccoli also contains beta-carotene, iron and potassium, and is high in bioflavonoids and other antioxidants. Iron is essential for the production of hemoglobin, the oxygen carrying pigment in red blood cells, and myoglobin, a similar pigment which stores oxygen in your muscles.

Pumpkin - a good source of beta-carotene and vitamin E. Pumpkin seeds are rich in iron, phosphorus, potassium, magnesium and zinc. Phosphorus is essential to the release of energy in cells, and also the transportation and absorption of many essential nutrients. Magnesium has an important role to play in healthy nerve transmission and muscle contraction, and zinc aids the action of many enzymes, including those involved in the destruction of free radicals.

Parsnip - a useful source of starch and fiber, parsnips provide a good alternative to potatoes. They also contain antioxidants in the form of vitamin C and vitamin E.

Spinach - a rich source of carotenoids, including beta-carotene and lutein, which are powerful antioxidants. Also contains vitamin C and potassium.

Collard Greens - a good source of omega-3 essential fatty acids which have anti-inflammatory properties.

Kale - a good source of iron, calcium, vitamin C and beta-carotene.

Cabbage - green varieties of cabbage offer a rich source of vitamin C and vitamin K, and a good source of vitamin E and potassium.

Honey

Honey contains glucose which provides your body with an instantly useable form of fuel.

Maple Syrup or Agave Syrup

Syrup can be used in addition to honey to add to the carbohydrate content or in place of honey to provide a different flavor. Maple syrup contains zinc and manganese, both known to help boost the immune system, and agave syrup provides a slower release of energy than honey and fruit, making it a useful energy source for endurance sports. Another benefit of agave is its anti-inflammatory properties.

Oatmeal

Oatmeal provides a slow release of energy, helping to keep you going for longer, and also contains protein to promote muscle growth and repair.

Cooked Rice

Cooked rice provides an alternative to oatmeal, also containing slow energy release carbohydrates and protein.

A carbohydrate-rich smoothie can provide a pre-training boost to your glycogen stores and it can also provide a glycogen replenishing "recovery" boost after an intense training session. Adding carbohydrates to a smoothie is a great way to fuel your performance or aid your recovery without the need to eat bulky meals that might lead to discomfort. As an example, 50 gram carbohydrate add-ons include:

Two tablespoons of honey

One small pot of yogurt

Two large bananas

One large mango

Three or four apples

Three or four pears

One glass of pure orange juice

175 grams of cooked brown rice

Fat

Contrary to popular belief, we all need fat in our diet. Around 30 percent of an active triathlete's daily diet should be fat, but it must be a healthy source of fat. Not all fats are equal. Like carbohydrates, fats also provide energy. In fact, fats yield nine calories per gram compared to only four calories per gram for carbohydrates. However, fat is a much slower source of energy so when you are training hard, your body relies on your glycogen stores to fuel your performance by providing a faster release of energy. During longer duration, steadier-paced training sessions or events, your body aims to conserve as much of its glycogen reserves as possible by using some of its fat stores for energy instead.

Fats can be split into two main groups:

Saturated fats: these are the unhealthy fats found in foods such as butter, cheese, and fatty meats.

Unsaturated fats: these are the healthier fats found in vegetable oils, fish oils, nuts, seeds and avocados.

Your body can make its own fat from excess carbohydrates and protein in your diet but it cannot manufacture certain essential unsaturated fats, meaning that the foods you eat are your body's only supply. The essential fatty acids are omega-3, found in green leafy vegetables and some vegetable oils, and omega-6, found in vegetable oils such as olive oil and sunflower oil. Fats act as a carrier for fat-soluble vitamins, including vitamins A, D, K, and E, and they provide insulation and protection for your body.

"Healthy fat" smoothie ingredients include:

Flax seeds

Also known as linseeds, flax seeds are high in omega-3 essential fatty acids and they also contain B vitamins, magnesium and manganese. B vitamins are involved in the release of energy from food, magnesium plays an important role in muscle contraction, and manganese is a vital component of many enzymes involved in energy production.

Peanut butter

Peanuts are high in healthy unsaturated fat, making them high in energy giving calories. They also contain B vitamins, phosphorus, iron, copper, potassium and vitamin E. Copper helps to protect against free radical damage and plays an important role in helping the body to absorb iron from food.

Almond butter

Almonds are also a good source of vitamin E and antioxidants to give your immune system a boost. They may also help to relieve leg cramps, including night cramps, a common complaint in endurance sports. Leg cramps are the result of fatigue and an electrolyte imbalance. Adding peanut or almond butter to a smoothie is an effective way to restore and then maintain the balance.

Protein

Protein is essentially the body's muscle-builder. It can be used as a source of energy but this would only be the case if your body's glycogen stores were totally depleted. However, protein is essential for healthy tissue growth and repair, and is of particular value to triathletes who may suffer soft tissue damage through the repetitive wear and tear of the sport. Green leafy vegetables are a valuable source of protein making a green smoothie a convenient way to boost protein intake.

Protein-rich smoothie ingredients include:

Milk

Low-fat milk is a source of high quality protein, also calcium, zinc and phosphorus.

Non-fat yogurt

Yogurt offers another good source of calcium and phosphorus, and adds a creamy texture to a smoothie without adding fat.

Oatmeal

Oatmeal provides complex carbohydrates and is also relatively high in protein content.

Benefits of Smoothies for Triathletes

Smoothies provide a convenient method of consuming the quality calories required to fuel performance. A pre-training session or pre-event smoothie provides the carbohydrates needed for energy and also the fluids needed for essential hydration without overloading the stomach. A post-training session or post-event smoothie helps to replenish your body's glycogen stores and to promote muscle repair after an intense effort. This helps to ensure that your glycogen stores are kept topped up for every performance, whether in day-to-day training or in competition.

Pre-training Smoothie

Base ingredients for a typical pre-training smoothie might include:

Fruits of your choice - fresh or frozen fruits provide carbohydrates for energy, and a rich source of health boosting antioxidants. The moderately slow release of energy provided by the fructose in fruits helps to keep you going for longer.

Cooked oatmeal - adding oatmeal provides a further source of carbohydrate and a slow release of energy. It is also relatively high in protein, helping to promote muscle growth and repair.

Honey - honey provides energy boosting simple carbohydrates in the form of glucose and fructose.

Water or ice cubes - adding water or ice changes the consistency of the smoothie, so the exact amount required is a matter of personal choice. More liquid means more hydration but it can also mean greater potential for sloshing around in your stomach. A process of trial and error is needed to discover the consistency that works best for you. Fruit juice can also provide additional liquid, extra vitamin C and more flavor, allowing you to alter the consistency without diluting the carbohydrate value. Any added juices should always be 100 percent fruit juice.

A smoothie containing fruit, honey, oats and dairy consumed around 60 to 90 minutes before training is an effective combination, providing a moderately fast-acting source of energy which is accelerated by the blending process. "Hobby" triathletes training for short-distance events will find that a smoothie containing only the base ingredients will satisfy their needs, but if training intensely with the goal of improving your performance, additional carbohydrates will be required. As a general rule, you should add 0.45 grams of carbohydrate per each pound of body weight before a moderate intensity session of two to four hours and 0.68 grams of carbohydrates per pound of body weight before an intense session of four or more hours.

Post-training Smoothie

A smoothie consumed within the 30 minute post-ride glycogen window is an effective way to help your body recover from your efforts and also replenish depleted glycogen stores so that you'll be fully energized for your next session. During this window, the enzymes in your body responsible for making glycogen are more active, meaning that glycogen stores can be replenished faster by consuming carbohydrate-rich foods. However, it's not unusual to find that you are not at all hungry immediately after hard training and a full meal is not something you can stomach. A "recovery" smoothie provides a readily digestible alternative. Adding a small amount of protein to create a 3:1 ratio of carbohydrates to protein provides an ideal recovery combination. Protein stimulates the action of insulin which boosts glycogen replacement by aiding the transportation of glucose from the blood to the muscles.

The ideal ingredient combination in a post-training smoothie might include:

Fruits of your choice - any fruit combination will provide the carbohydrates you need to replenish your glycogen stores so it comes down to personal taste. Fruits with antioxidant properties can help to reduce the effects of any muscular damage.

Honey -honey provides instantly useable carbohydrates to give your post-training energy levels a lift. It also adds sweetness to a smoothie which can make it more appealing when you are not feeling hungry.

Milk or Yogurt - milk provides whey protein and casein protein. Whey is a fast acting protein which helps to reduce the effects of muscle damage immediately after an intense training session or race, and casein is a slow acting protein which helps to continue the repair process long after the event. **Whey powder** provides a convenient alternative source of protein.

Flax seeds, peanut butter, or almond butter can also provide additional "healthy" fat and flavor to increase the appeal to your taste buds.

Fluids and Hydration

Adequate hydration is essential at all times and of particular importance to long-distance triathletes. Fluids must be carried with you on your bike ride and also on your run so that small, frequent sips can be taken to help maintain hydration levels without overloading your stomach. This can be in the form of plain water or a drink specially formulated for sport containing a ratio of four grams of carbohydrate to one gram of protein.

Remaining hydrated during a training session or race is essential as fluid in your blood transports glucose to the working muscles and takes away the metabolic by-products. A smoothie provides a practical way to top up and replenish essential fluids and the water content of the fruits included in your smoothie can significantly increase the overall fluid content.

Melon - 94 percent water

Grapefruit - 91 percent water

Strawberries - 89 percent water

Oranges - 86 percent water

Peaches - 86 percent water

Apples - 84 percent water

Grapes - 79 percent water

Bananas - 71 percent water

Nutritious *and* Delicious

There are virtually no limits in terms of choosing smoothie ingredients other than in your imagination. Experimentation is the only way to discover the flavor combinations that work best for you. The fresher your ingredients, the more nutritional value they hold, but it is worth noting that frozen produce can represent a good choice when fresh foods may have spent a little longer than ideal on the grocery store shelf. Organic produce will generally offer a healthier choice, but non-organic produce still provides the nutrients you need to fuel your body for multi-sport endurance activities and to boost your overall health.

Adding fresh herbs to a green smoothie can add a flavorsome twist and also boost the nutritional benefits. Popular choices include:

Parsley - one cup of parsley contains 2 grams of protein. It is also rich in calcium and provides iron, copper, magnesium, potassium, zinc, phosphorus, beta-carotene and vitamin C.

Dill – adds a sweet flavor to a smoothie and contains calcium, iron, manganese, vitamin C, and beta-carotene.

Sorrel - provides iron, magnesium and calcium.

Basil - provides beta-carotene, iron, potassium, copper, manganese and magnesium

Coriander - provides a mild, peppery flavor along with anti-inflammatory properties, vitamin C, iron and magnesium.

Tea - adding tea in moderation can boost the antioxidant content. Herbal teas can also add flavor.

Chocolate - all types of chocolate contain potassium, and varieties with over 50 percent cocoa solids contain iron and magnesium. The caffeine content of chocolate can also help to increase your alertness. However, it is also high in fats and sugar.

Tried and tested smoothie recipes are a great way to get started and then as you begin to discover the nutrient and flavor combinations that appeal to you most, you can begin to experiment with your own creations. Finding time to swim, cycle and run can make finding time to cook and eat a challenge. Smoothies provide a quick and convenient way to boost your body's intake of the nutrients it needs to perform at its best in training and in competition … energizing your muscles, your mind and your taste buds!

General Information about Your Smoothies

These smoothies are divided into 3 categories, each designed to meet the nutritional needs of triathletes in three moments:

Before the race - for races lasting 2 to 4 hours;

Before the race - for races lasting 4 or more hours;

Post-race smoothies.

The great majority of the ingredients in these recipes has a low Glycemic Index.

When the recipes call for fruit juice, always choose one that is made of pure fruit.

If you can't find the fresh fruit you need for a recipe, feel free to replace it with frozen. Frozen fruits have the same nutritional content as the corresponding fresh fruits.

You can adjust the consistency of your smoothie adding some ice cubes to the recipe before blending and/or straining before serving.

Pre-race smoothies - for races lasting 2 to 4 hours

These smoothies were developed to provide an adequate amount of Carbohydrates for a 150 pounds person. You can adjust the amount of carbohydrates by adding, for each extra 5 pounds of your body weight, one of the following:

- 2 tsps. of oatmeal;
- ½ tsp. of honey;
- 1 tbsp. of flax seed;
- 2 tsps. of high fiber cereal;
- ¼ tbsp. of fruit jam;
- 1 tsp. of seeded raisins;
- ½ tbsp. of dried apricots;
- 3 ½ tbsps. of reduced fat milk;
- 2 ½ tbsps. of low fat yogurt.

1. Mango and Banana Smoothie

Preparation time	5 minutes
Ready time	5 minutes
Serves	1
Serving quantity/unit	500 G / 18 Ounces
Calories	332 Cal
Total Fat	1g
Cholesterol	5 mg
Sodium	193 mg
Total Carbohydrates	70 g
Dietary fibers	5 g
Sugars	58 g
Protein	16 g

Prepare your smoothie combining the following ingredients in a food processor:

- 1 cup of mango
- ½ cup of sliced banana
- 1 cup of fat free yogurt
- 1 tsp. of honey

2. Creamy Watermelon and Raisins Smoothie

Preparation time	5 minutes
Ready time	5 minutes
Serves	1
Serving quantity/unit	250 G / 9 Ounces
Calories	262 Cal
Total Fat	1 g
Cholesterol	0 mg
Sodium	10 mg
Total Carbohydrates	69 g
Dietary fibers	3g
Sugars	52 g
Protein	3 g

Prepare your smoothie combining the following ingredients in a food processor:

2 cups of cubed watermelon

1/3 cup of raisins

½ cup of fat free cream cheese

3. Pear, Oats and Almond Milk Smoothie

Preparation time	5 minutes
Ready time	5 minutes
Serves	1
Serving quantity/unit	470 G / 17 Ounces
Calories	316 Cal
Total Fat	4 g
Cholesterol	0 mg
Sodium	79 mg
Total Carbohydrates	69 g
Dietary fibers	8 g
Sugars	38 g
Protein	6 g

Prepare your smoothie combining the following ingredients in a food processor:

- 1 cup of sliced pear
- ¾ cup of oats
- ½ cup of almond milk
- 1 tbsp. of honey

4. Cucumber, Strawberry and Banana Smoothie

Preparation time	5 minutes
Ready time	5 minutes
Serves	1
Serving quantity/unit	400 G / 14 Ounces
Calories	274 Cal
Total Fat	1 g
Cholesterol	0 mg
Sodium	6 mg
Total Carbohydrates	69 g
Dietary fibers	8 g
Sugars	44 g
Protein	4g

Prepare your smoothie combining the following ingredients in a food processor:

- ¾ cup of cucumber
- 1 cup of sliced strawberries
- 1 cup of sliced banana
- 1 tbsp. of oats
- 1 tbsp. of honey

Cucumber is a very good source of vitamin K and minerals such as potassium but it is also important for its hydration potential since it has a water proportion of 95%.

5. Fruit Smoothie with Spinach

Preparation time	5 minutes
Ready time	5 minutes
Serves	1
Serving quantity/unit	500 G / 18 Ounces
Calories	281 Cal
Total Fat	1 g
Cholesterol	0 mg
Sodium	66 mg
Total Carbohydrates	68 g
Dietary fibers	3g
Sugars	62 g
Protein	3 g

Prepare your smoothie combining the following ingredients in a food processor:

- 1 ½ cups of spinach
- ¾ cup of cubed melon
- ¾ cup of grapes
- 1 cup of mixed fruit juice
- 1 tbsp. of honey

6. Apple, Pineapple and Cinnamon Smoothie

Preparation time	5 minutes
Ready time	5 minutes
Serves	1
Serving quantity/unit	500 G / 18 Ounces
Calories	323 Cal
Total Fat	2 g
Cholesterol	4 mg
Sodium	81 mg
Total Carbohydrates	70 g
Dietary fibers	8 g
Sugars	48 g
Protein	10 g

Prepare your smoothie combining the following ingredients in a food processor:

- 1 cup of sliced apple
- ¾ cup of cubed pineapple
- ¼ cup of oats
- ¾ cup of fat free milk
- 2 ½ tbsps. of apple jam
- 1 tsp. of cinnamon

7. Peach, Papaya and Vanilla Smoothie

Preparation time	5 minutes
Ready time	5 minutes
Serves	1
Serving quantity/unit	500 G / 18 Ounces
Calories	296 Cal
Total Fat	0 g
Cholesterol	0 mg
Sodium	89 mg
Total Carbohydrates	68 g
Dietary fibers	7g
Sugars	67 g
Protein	6 g

Prepare your smoothie combining the following ingredients in a food processor:

- ½ cup of sliced peach
- ¼ cup of dried apricots
- ¾ cup of cubed papaya
- 1 cup of vanilla flavored soy milk
- 1 ½ tsps. of honey

8. Peach and Apricot Smoothie

Preparation time	5 minutes
Ready time	5 minutes
Serves	1
Serving quantity/unit	500 G / 18 Ounces
Calories	296 Cal
Total Fat	0 g
Cholesterol	0 mg
Sodium	89 mg
Total Carbohydrates	68 g
Dietary fibers	7g
Sugars	67 g
Protein	6 g

Prepare your smoothie combining the following ingredients in a food processor:

- ¾ cup of sliced peach
- ½ cup of dried apricots
- ½ cup of fat free milk
- 1 tsp. of honey

9. Cherry and Papaya Smoothie

Preparation time	5 minutes
Ready time	5 minutes
Serves	1
Serving quantity/unit	500 G / 18 Ounces
Calories	302 Cal
Total Fat	2g
Cholesterol	5 mg
Sodium	76 mg
Total Carbohydrates	69 g
Dietary fibers	8 g
Sugars	55g
Protein	8g

Prepare your smoothie combining the following ingredients in a food processor:

- 1 cup of cherries
- ½ cup of papaya
- ½ cup of low fat cherry yogurt

10. Grape and Raisins Smoothie

Preparation time	5 minutes
Ready time	5 minutes
Serves	1
Serving quantity/unit	350 G / 12 Ounces
Calories	282 Cal
Total Fat	2g
Cholesterol	0mg
Sodium	78mg
Total Carbohydrates	70 g
Dietary fibers	3g
Sugars	60 g
Protein	3g

Prepare your smoothie combining the following ingredients in a food processor:

- 2 ¼ cup of grapes
- ¼ cup of raisins
- ½ cup of almond milk

Pre-race smoothies - for races lasting 4 or more hours

Like the previous smoothies, these were also designed to provide an adequate amount of Carbohydrates to a 150 pounds person. If you weight more than this, consider adjusting the amount of carbohydrates through the addition, by each extra 5 pounds of body weight, of one of the following.

- 1 tbsp. of oatmeal;
- ¾ tsp. of honey;
- 1 ½ tbsps. of flax seed;
- 1 tbsp. of high fiber cereal;
- 1 tsp. of fruit jam;
- 1 ½ tsps. of seeded raisins;
- 1 tbsp. of dried apricots;
- 5 tbsps. of reduced fat milk;
- 3 tbsps. of low fat yogurt.

11. Banana and Blueberries Smoothie

Preparation time	5 minutes
Ready time	5 minutes
Serves	1
Serving quantity/unit	500 G / 18 Ounces
Calories	496 Cal
Total Fat	5 g
Cholesterol	4 mg
Sodium	84 mg
Total Carbohydrates	103 g
Dietary fibers	14 g
Sugars	39 g
Protein	17 g

Prepare your smoothie combining the following ingredients in a food processor:

- 1 cup of sliced banana
- ¾ cup of blueberries
- ¾ cup of oats
- ¾ cup of fat free milk
- 1 tsp. of cinnamon

12. Pear and Kiwi Smoothie

Preparation time	5 minutes
Ready time	5 minutes
Serves	1
Serving quantity/unit	600 G /21 Ounces
Calories	467 Cal
Total Fat	2 g
Cholesterol	4 mg
Sodium	148 mg
Total Carbohydrates	103 g
Dietary fibers	10 g
Sugars	60 g
Protein	15 g

Prepare your smoothie combining the following ingredients in a food processor:

- ¾ cup of sliced pear
- ½ cup of kiwi
- ½ cup of sliced banana
- ½ cup of cooked brown rice
- ¾ cup of fat free yogurt
- 1 tbsp. of honey

13. Plum, Guava and Rice Milk Smoothie

Preparation time	5 minutes
Ready time	5 minutes
Serves	1
Serving quantity/unit	450 G / 16 Ounces
Calories	468 Cal
Total Fat	4 g
Cholesterol	0 mg
Sodium	48 mg
Total Carbohydrates	104 g
Dietary fibers	11g
Sugars	37 g
Protein	7 g

Prepare your smoothie combining the following ingredients in a food processor:

- ¾ cup of plums
- ¾ cup of guava
- 4 tbsps. of oats
- ½ cup rice milk
- 2 tbsps. of strawberry jam
- 1 ½ tsps. of honey

14. Loquat and Whole Wheat Cookies Smoothie

Preparation time	5 minutes
Ready time	5 minutes
Serves	1
Serving quantity/unit	400 G / 14 Ounce
Calories	513 Cal
Total Fat	8 g
Cholesterol	0 mg
Sodium	374 mg
Total Carbohydrates	103 g
Dietary fibers	5g
Sugars	26 g
Protein	11g

Prepare your smoothie combining the following ingredients in a food processor:

- 1 cup of loquats
- 10 whole wheat, plain, round biscuits
- ½ cup of fat free peach yogurt
- 2 ½ tsps. of honey

15. Raspberry and Apple Smoothie

Preparation time	5 minutes
Ready time	5 minutes
Serves	1
Serving quantity/unit	550 G / 19 Ounces
Calories	553 Cal
Total Fat	9 g
Cholesterol	0 mg
Sodium	134 mg
Total Carbohydrates	104 g
Dietary fibers	18g
Sugars	45 g
Protein	18g

Prepare your smoothie combining the following ingredients in a food processor:

- 1 cup of raspberries
- 1 cup of sliced apple
- ¾ cup of oatmeal
- 1 cup of soy milk
- 1 tbsp. of honey

16. Dried Figs and Greek yogurt Smoothie

Preparation time	5 minutes
Ready time	5 minutes
Serves	1
Serving quantity/unit	350 G / 12 Ounces
Calories	559 Cal
Total Fat	8 g
Cholesterol	10 mg
Sodium	205 mg
Total Carbohydrates	102 g
Dietary fibers	11 g
Sugars	70 g
Protein	25g

Prepare your smoothie combining the following ingredients in a food processor:

- ½ cup of dried figs
- 5 whole wheat, plain, round biscuits
- ½ tbsp. of honey
- 1 7oz container of Greek yogurt

17. Pumpkin, Mango and Peach Smoothie

Preparation time	5 minutes
Ready time	5 minutes
Serves	1
Serving quantity/unit	600 G / 21 Ounces
Calories	405 Cal
Total Fat	2 g
Cholesterol	0 mg
Sodium	30 mg
Total Carbohydrates	102 g
Dietary fibers	9 g
Sugars	80 g
Protein	4 g

Prepare your smoothie combining the following ingredients in a food processor:

- ¾ cup of cooked pumpkin
- ¾ cup of mango
- 1 cup of peach juice
- 2 tbsps. of oats
- 1 tsp. of pumpkin pie spice
- 1 ½ tbsps. of honey

Pumpkin is a vital source of Vitamin A and it is also a very good source of vitamin K, E and pantothenic acid. Important amounts of essential minerals such as iron, magnesium, potassium, copper and manganese are also provided when eating this vegetable.

18. Melon, Watermelon and Strawberry yogurt Smoothie

Preparation time	5 minutes
Ready time	5 minutes
Serves	1
Serving quantity/unit	700 G / 25 Ounces
Calories	451 Cal
Total Fat	3 g
Cholesterol	8 mg
Sodium	150 mg
Total Carbohydrates	104g
Dietary fibers	7g
Sugars	90g
Protein	12g

Prepare your smoothie combining the following ingredients in a food processor:

- 1 ¼ cups of cubed watermelon
- 2 cups of cubed melon
- ¼ cup of prunes
- ¾ cup of low fat strawberry yogurt
- 1 tsp. of honey

19. Pineapple and Banana Smoothie

Preparation time	5 minutes
Ready time	5 minutes
Serves	1
Serving quantity/unit	700 G / 24 Ounces
Calories	454 Cal
Total Fat	4g
Cholesterol	0 mg
Sodium	99 mg
Total Carbohydrates	104 g
Dietary fibers	11g
Sugars	65g
Protein	10g

Prepare your smoothie combining the following ingredients in a food processor:

- 2 cups of cubed pineapple
- 1 ½ cup of sliced banana
- ¾ cup of soy milk

20. Orange and Pomegranate Smoothie

Preparation time	5 minutes
Ready time	5 minutes
Serves	1
Serving quantity/unit	750 G / 26 Ounces
Calories	456 Cal
Total Fat	1g
Cholesterol	5 mg
Sodium	319 mg
Total Carbohydrates	104g
Dietary fibers	3g
Sugars	82g
Protein	13g

Prepare your smoothie combining the following ingredients in a food processor:

- 1 ¼ cups of fresh orange juice
- Seeds of 2 ½ medium pomegranates (around 150g/5ounces each)
- ¼ cup of fat free cream cheese
- ½ tsp. of honey

21. Cranberries and Guava Smoothie

Preparation time	5 minutes
Ready time	5 minutes
Serves	1
Serving quantity/unit	735 G / 26 Ounces
Calories	469 Cal
Total Fat	4g
Cholesterol	4 mg
Sodium	91 mg
Total Carbohydrates	105 g
Dietary fibers	28g
Sugars	65 g
Protein	16g

Prepare your smoothie combining the following ingredients in a food processor:

- 2 cups of cranberries
- 2 cups of guava
- 3 ½ tbsps. of raisins
- ¾ cup of fat free milk

Post-race smoothies

These smoothies constitute great combinations of carbohydrates and protein sources which will be essential to give your body the right nutrients, enhancing its recovery. Also in these recipes, if you weight more than 150 pounds, consider adjusting the nutritional content of your smoothie by adding, for each extra 5 pounds of body weight, one of these:

- 1 tbsp. of oatmeal;
- 1 tbsp. of almonds;
- 1 tbsp. of nuts mixture;
- 1 tbsp. of peanuts;
- 1 tbsp. of flaxseeds;
- 1tbsp. of sesame seeds;
- 2 tbsps. of milk;
- 2 tbsps. of yogurt.

22. Creamy Orange and Blackberry Smoothie

Preparation time	5 minutes
Ready time	5 minutes
Serves	1
Serving quantity/unit	550 G / 19 Ounces
Calories	407 Cal
Total Fat	4 g
Cholesterol	0 mg
Sodium	638 mg
Total Carbohydrates	74 g
Dietary fibers	10g
Sugars	46 g
Protein	23g

Prepare your smoothie combining the following ingredients in a food processor:

- 1 cup of orange juice
- 1 cup of blackberries
- 3 tbsps. of oats
- ½ cup of fat free cream cheese
- 1 tbsp. of honey

23. Pear and Vanilla Smoothie with Soy milk

Preparation time	5 minutes
Ready time	5 minutes
Serves	1
Serving quantity/unit	550 G / 19 Ounces
Calories	475 Cal
Total Fat	13 g
Cholesterol	22 mg
Sodium	183 mg
Total Carbohydrates	72 g
Dietary fibers	7g
Sugars	52 g
Protein	22g

Prepare your smoothie combining the following ingredients in a food processor:

- 1 cup of sliced peach
- ½ cup of sliced banana
- ¼ cup of almonds
- ½ cup of fat free ricotta cheese
- ½ cup of fat free milk
- 1 tbsp. of honey

24. Avocado and Lemon Smoothie

Preparation time	5 minutes
Ready time	5 minutes
Serves	1
Serving quantity/unit	500 G / 18 Ounces
Calories	574 Cal
Total Fat	27 g
Cholesterol	0 mg
Sodium	36 mg
Total Carbohydrates	72 g
Dietary fibers	14 g
Sugars	30 g
Protein	24 g

Prepare your smoothie combining the following ingredients in a food processor:

- ¾ cup of avocado
- ¼ cup of lemon juice
- ½ cup of oatmeal
- ¾ cup of tofu
- 1 ½ tbsps. of honey
- 2 ice cubes

25. Coconut and Melon Smoothie

Preparation time	5 minutes
Ready time	5 minutes
Serves	1
Serving quantity/unit	450 G / 16 Ounces
Calories	508 Cal
Total Fat	14 g
Cholesterol	12 mg
Sodium	197 mg
Total Carbohydrates	78 g
Dietary fibers	5 g
Sugars	64 g
Protein	22g

Prepare your smoothie combining the following ingredients in a food processor:

- 1 cup of cubed melon
- ½ cup of coconut meat
- 1 cup of coconut Greek yogurt
- 1 tbsp. of non-fat powdered milk
- 1 tbsp. of honey

26. Pear and Strawberry Smoothie

Preparation time	5 minutes
Ready time	5 minutes
Serves	1
Serving quantity/unit	500 G /18 Ounces
Calories	413 Cal
Total Fat	4 g
Cholesterol	10 mg
Sodium	147 mg
Total Carbohydrates	81 g
Dietary fibers	12 g
Sugars	60 g
Protein	22 g

Prepare your smoothie combining the following ingredients in a food processor:

- ¾ cup of sliced strawberries
- ¾ cup of sliced pear
- 1 cup of low fat strawberry yogurt
- 2 ½ tbsps. of nutritional yeast

27. Mango and Watermelon Smoothie

Preparation time	5 minutes
Ready time	5 minutes
Serves	1
Serving quantity/unit	500 G / 18 Ounces
Calories	473 Cal
Total Fat	9 g
Cholesterol	9 mg
Sodium	638 mg
Total Carbohydrates	68 g
Dietary fibers	10 g
Sugars	40 g
Protein	25g

Prepare your smoothie combining the following ingredients in a food processor:

- 1 cup of cubed watermelon
- 1 cup of mango
- ½ cup of fat free cream cheese
- 3 tbsps. of oats
- 2 tbsps. of flax seeds
- 1 tsp. of honey

28. Multi-fruit Smoothie with Collard greens

Preparation time	5 minutes
Ready time	5 minutes
Serves	1
Serving quantity/unit	550 G / 19 Ounces
Calories	364 Cal
Total Fat	1 g
Cholesterol	0 mg
Sodium	132 mg
Total Carbohydrates	72 g
Dietary fibers	11 g
Sugars	44 g
Protein	24 g

Prepare your smoothie combining the following ingredients in a food processor:

- 1 cup of collard greens
- 1 cup of sliced banana
- ½ cup of sliced apple
- ½ cup of sliced strawberries
- ½ cup of sliced pear
- ½ cup of fat free ricotta
- 2 ice cubes

Collard greens are a great source of essential nutrients. The portion of collards in this smoothie will provide you half of the daily recommended amount of vitamin A and twice as much of the daily requirements of vitamin K.

29. Grape and Banana Smoothie

Preparation time	5 minutes
Ready time	5 minutes
Serves	1
Serving quantity/unit	500 G / 18 Ounces
Calories	475 Cal
Total Fat	8 g
Cholesterol	10 mg
Sodium	198 mg
Total Carbohydrates	80 g
Dietary fibers	6 g
Sugars	47 g
Protein	24g

Prepare your smoothie combining the following ingredients in a food processor:

- 1 cup of grapes
- 1 cup of sliced banana
- 5 whole wheat, plain, round biscuits
- 1 cup of Greek yogurt

30. Papaya and Passion-fruit Smoothie with Carrot

Preparation time	5 minutes
Ready time	5 minutes
Serves	1
Serving quantity/unit	550 G / 19 Ounces
Calories	432 Cal
Total Fat	12 g
Cholesterol	0 mg
Sodium	151 mg
Total Carbohydrates	69 g
Dietary fibers	25g
Sugars	36 g
Protein	22g

Prepare your smoothie combining the following ingredients in a food processor:

- ½ cup of cubed papaya
- ¾ cup of passion-fruit pulp
- 1 cup of carrots
- ¾ cup of tofu
- 1 tbsp. of almonds
- 1 tsp. of honey

31. Lemon and Strawberry Smoothie

Preparation time	5 minutes
Ready time	5 minutes
Serves	1
Serving quantity/unit	680 G /24 Ounces
Calories	399 Cal
Total Fat	1g
Cholesterol	40mg
Sodium	264mg
Total Carbohydrates	171g
Dietary fibers	6g
Sugars	25g
Protein	22g

Prepare your smoothie combining the following ingredients in a food processor:

- 2 cups of sliced strawberries
- ½ cup of lemon juice
- 1 tbsp. of strawberry jam
- 1 cup of fat free ricotta

32. Quince and Apple Smoothie

Preparation time	5 minutes
Ready time	5 minutes
Serves	1
Serving quantity/unit	620 G / 22 Ounces
Calories	395 Cal
Total Fat	4g
Cholesterol	19mg
Sodium	690mg
Total Carbohydrates	72g
Dietary fibers	9g
Sugars	41g
Protein	22g

Prepare your smoothie combining the following ingredients in a food processor:

- 2 ½ cups of sliced apple
- 1 seeded quince (around 100 g)
- ½ cup of milk
- ½ cup of fat free cream cheese
- 1 tsp. of honey
- 1 tsp. of ginger

33. Grape and Pear Smoothie

Preparation time	5 minutes
Ready time	5 minutes
Serves	1
Serving quantity/unit	540 G / 19 Ounces
Calories	386 Cal
Total Fat	1 g
Cholesterol	40 mg
Sodium	264 mg
Total Carbohydrates	69g
Dietary fibers	6g
Sugars	46 g
Protein	21 g

Prepare your smoothie combining the following ingredients in a food processor:

- 1 cup of pear
- 1 ½ cups of grapes
- 1 cup of fat free ricotta

34. Kiwi, Raspberry and Pomegranate Smoothie

Preparation time	5 minutes
Ready time	5 minutes
Serves	1
Serving quantity/unit	570 G / 20 Ounces
Calories	389 Cal
Total Fat	5g
Cholesterol	9mg
Sodium	61 mg
Total Carbohydrates	72g
Dietary fibers	10g
Sugars	52 g
Protein	21g

Prepare your smoothie combining the following ingredients in a food processor:

- 1 cup of kiwi
- ½ cup of raspberries
- Seeds of 1 pomegranate (around 150g/5ounces)
- ¾ cup of Greek yogurt
- 1 tsp. of honey

35. Passion fruit and Loquat Smoothie

Preparation time	5 minutes
Ready time	5 minutes
Serves	1
Serving quantity/unit	500 G / 18 Ounces
Calories	542 Cal
Total Fat	25g
Cholesterol	4mg
Sodium	128mg
Total Carbohydrates	70g
Dietary fibers	26g
Sugars	31g
Protein	21g

Prepare your smoothie combining the following ingredients in a food processor:

- ¾ cup of passion-fruit
- ½ cup of loquats
- ¾ cup of fat free milk
- ½ cup of almonds

Exclusive Bonus Download: Athletic Training

Download your bonus, please visit the download link above from your PC or MAC. To open PDF files, visit http://get.adobe.com/reader/ to download the reader if it's not already installed on your PC or Mac. To open ZIP files, you may need to download WinZip from http://www.winzip.com. This download is for PC or Mac ONLY and might not be downloadable to kindle.

Always wanted to be a world class athlete? Here is everything you need to know on how to reach the peaks of performance!

Do you ever envy those people who are ace athletes without appearing to put any effort into it at all?

Without the right tools and information, it could take you years to figure out the secrets to achieving peak performance. Instead of spending a fortune on so-called experts or knocking yourself out with the old trial and error method, there is an easier way to learn how to achieve success in athletics the way you've always dreamed.

Introducing... Athletic Training!

Everything you need to know about becoming a great athlete is included in this special report:

- Secrets to peak performance
- Achieving balance
- Purpose and performance
- Planning
- Training regimens
- Goal setting
- Training your whole body
- Strength training

I leave absolutely nothing out! Everything that I learned in order to improve to learn how to become an ace athlete, I show you.

No stone is left unturned in this comprehensive report! You won't want to miss out on this!

Visit the URL above to download this guide and start achieving your weight loss and fitness goals NOW

One Last Thing...

Thank you so much for reading my book. I hope you really liked it. As you probably know, many people look at the reviews on Amazon before they decide to purchase a book. If you liked the book, could you please take a minute to leave a review with your feedback? 60 seconds is all I'm asking for, and it would mean the world to me.

✶✶✶✶✶✶

Books by This Author

The Smoothies for Runners Book

Juices for Runners

Smoothies for Cyclists

Juices for Cyclists

Paleo Diet for Cyclists

Smoothies for Triathletes

Juices for Triathletes

Paleo Diet for Triathletes

Smoothies for Strength

Juices for Strength

Paleo Diet for Strength

Paleo Diet Smoothies for Strength

Smoothies for Golfers

Juices for Golfers

About the Author

Lars Andersen is a sports author, nutritional researcher and fitness enthusiast. In his spare time he participates in competitive running, swimming and cycling events and enjoys hiking with his two border collies.

Lars Andersen

Published by Nordic Standard Publishing

Atlanta, Georgia USA

NORDICSTANDARD
PUBLISHING

Lars Andersen

16287916R00046

Printed in Poland
by Amazon Fulfillment
Poland Sp. z o.o., Wrocław